Good First Foods

Sara Lewis

hamlyn

This book is dedicated to my children Alice and William

First published in Great Britain in 2002 by
Hamlyn, a division of Octopus Publishing Group Ltd
2–4 Heron Quays, London E14 4JP

ISBN 0 600 60458 6

A CIP catalogue record for this book is available from the British
Library

Printed and bound in China

10 9 8 7 6 5 4 3 2 1

Some of this material appeared in *Veggie Food for Kids* also
published by Hamlyn

The Author
Sara Lewis has been the cookery editor for *Practical Parenting*
magazine for the last 11 years. She has two young children,
one of whom is vegetarian, so she knows the joys and frustrations
of cooking for children with different tastes. She writes
regularly for vegetarian magazines and has written two books
on feeding children.

NOTES
Both metric and imperial measurements have been given
in all recipes. Use one set of measurements only, and
not a mixture of both.

Standard level spoon measurements are used in all recipes.
1 tablespoon = one 15 ml spoon
1 teaspoon = one 5 ml spoon

Eggs should be large unless otherwise stated.

Milk should be full fat unless otherwise stated.

This book includes dishes made with nuts and nut derivatives.
It is advisable for those with known allergic reactions to nuts
and nut derivatives and those who may be potentially vulnerable
to these allergies to avoid dishes made with nuts and nut oils.
It is also prudent to check the labels of pre-prepared ingredients
for the possible inclusion of nut derivatives.

Fresh herbs should be used, unless otherwise stated. If unavailable,
use dried herbs as an alternative, but halve the quantities stated.

Ovens should be preheated to the specified temperature
– if using a fan-assisted oven, follow the manufacturer's instructions
for adjusting the time and the temperature.

Vegetarians should look for the 'V' symbol on a cheese to ensure
it is made with vegetarian rennet.

Contents

Introduction

As parents we all want to do the best for our children and that includes the foods we offer them. These are vital, not just to show how much we care, but for their growth and well-being too. Just as there are critical periods for learning to walk, speak and recognize people, there seems to be a critical period for the development of taste preferences too.

Up to now milk has provided everything that your baby has required to stay healthy, but from four to six months she will begin to need additional foods to supplement her changing nutritional needs. Those first mini-spoonfuls of ultra-smooth purée herald the beginning of a new and exciting phase in your baby's life. This is a period of great discovery, but it is a good idea to give your baby time to adjust to this new way of receiving nourishment, especially in the first few weeks of weaning.

Knowing what foods and when to give them are crucial. First foods need to be completely smooth and easy to digest, so there is a detailed section in this book that not only includes recipes for your baby, but lots of tips on safe food preparation and storage too.

Some babies relish this new stage, while others prefer to wait. Some like the same food over and over again, others are happy to try new tastes and quickly move on to more varied and coarser purées. Each baby is an individual and, unless you already have children, this is new to both of you. Be guided by your baby and don't try to keep up with what your friends are doing with their own children – life is not a race after all.

Once weaning is well established, your baby's diet can quickly broaden and there are lots of recipes to tempt her. By the time she is approaching her first birthday, your feeding routine should be well established, your baby may even have begun to feed herself and you will be able to share an increasing number of family meals together.

This book is packed with practical and helpful advice on everything you need to know for feeding your baby in her first year – when to begin weaning, what foods to offer and at what stage, tips on batch cooking to help save time, plus lots of easy and tasty recipes to offer her as she changes from a tiny baby to a happy adventurous toddler.

The importance of milk

In the early months, the only food a baby requires to meet all his nutritional needs is milk — either breast or formula. All babies are born with a store of iron to last for the first six months and this is supplemented, to an extent, by the milk too. Breastfeeding gives your baby the best start in life and is the ideal food and drink. It contains all the nutrients he needs in the right proportions, as well as many antibodies which help fight infections. The high levels of fatty acids also protect a

baby susceptible to allergies. Iron levels are low in breast milk, but they are in a readily absorbed form and combine with your baby's iron store to provide all his needs for the first six months. Breast milk can adjust if your baby is premature, alter as your baby grows and his needs change and even dilute in hot weather to satisfy his thirst. Breastfeeding is sterile, free and always ready at the right temperature, virtually on demand. Like any new skill, breastfeeding can be difficult to master, especially in the early days. Do persevere if you can and don't be afraid to seek advice from your midwife, health visitor or breastfeeding counsellor. Continue until your baby is six weeks, six months or one year old, or until you and your baby are ready to stop.

Formula milk

Powdered cow's milk used in formulas is specially modified to be as close to the nutritional composition of breast milk as possible and fortified with vitamins and minerals. Whey-based formulas are given to newborn babies, while follow-on milks have a higher proportion of casein to whey and are suited to hungrier babies over six months. Make up formula feeds with previously boiled water and store in the refrigerator until

required. Do not use water that has been repeatedly boiled, softened water or bottled water, as they can be high in some mineral salts. Continue with formula milk feeds until your baby is 12 months, then progress to full-fat cow's milk.

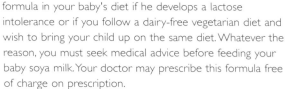

Soya-based infant formula

You may need to include a soya-based formula in your baby's diet if he develops a lactose intolerance or if you follow a dairy-free vegetarian diet and wish to bring your child up on the same diet. Whatever the reason, you must seek medical advice before feeding your baby soya milk. Your doctor may prescribe this formula free of charge on prescription.

Unlike other milks, soya does not contain sugar and is often sweetened with glucose syrup, which can be detrimental to teeth. Some soya formulas also contain small levels of aluminium and so are unsuitable for premature babies or those suffering from kidney problems. Do not give babies unmodified (or carton) soya milks before they are two years old.

Goat's milk

Suitable to use from birth, goat's milk infant formula can be less allergenic than cow's milk formula, as it is more easily digested. Ask your health professional or doctor about 'Nanny' infant formula. Do not give full-fat fresh goat's milk as a main drink to babies until they are over 12 months and then only if it is pasteurized.

Cow's milk

A good source of energy, protein, and vitamins and minerals, cow's milk is especially important for calcium, which is essential for growing teeth and bones. It can be added to cooking from six months, but should not be given as a drink to babies under 12 months.

What about other drinks?

Breastfed babies of less than three to four months do not need drinks other than breast milk, even in hot weather, as breast milk adapts naturally to become more thirst quenching when required. In the early days of breastfeeding it is also better to offer only breast milk so that mother and baby can establish a good feeding routine – the more a baby feeds, the more milk will be produced.

From six weeks or so, offer cooled, boiled water to babies fed on formula milk. Don't be tempted to add flavourings or sweeteners. A thirsty infant will happily drink water. Just as when making up formula feeds, use freshly drawn and boiled water, rather than water that has been repeatedly boiled, and do not give babies water from a tap fitted with a water softener. Avoid sparkling bottled water or still water with a high mineral content – often known as 'natural mineral water'. Check for suitable brands with your Health Visitor. If you do

decide to give bottled water, it will still need to be boiled and cooled for babies up to six months.

As your baby grows, you may want to offer different drinks too, but try to get into the habit of reading labels. Some baby herbal drinks may contain more sugar than you'd realize and it may be listed not just

as sugar, but as sucrose, glucose, glucose syrup, fructose, maltose, maltodextrin or corn syrup. Even though the packaging of a fruit juice style drink may feature cartoon characters it may be unsuitable for children under one year old. Artificial sweeteners, such as aspartame, saccharin or acesulfame-K are not designed for babies. Unsweetened fruit juices may be given to older babies between nine and twelve months if diluted 1 part juice to 10 parts water.

Introducing a beaker

Try to introduce a beaker to a baby from five to six months at meal times. To begin with, choose a small one that has tiny holes so that the drink does not come out too fast. Offer a little cooled boiled water, formula or breast milk. As your baby gets used to drinking from a beaker, progress to one with handles so that he can help to feed himself. Buy one with an anti-leak lid – invaluable for reducing spillage. Aim to move on to a beaker completely by the time your child is one year old or to limit using a bottle to the last milk drink of the day only. If your baby is used to a bottle, comfort sucking can be a hard habit to break, so trying alternating between a bottle and beaker.

Avoid giving fruit juices, even unsweetened ones, in a bottle as the prolonged sucking on juice can result in tooth decay. Offer juices in a beaker at meal times and try to resist the temptation to give a fractious baby a bottle to drink when out in the pushchair unless filled only with water.

First foods

The introduction of the first few ultra-smooth baby purées signals the start of a new and exciting landmark in your baby's development.

What is weaning?

Weaning, also called 'mixed feeding' or 'solid feeding', is the process that begins with giving tiny spoonfuls of ultra-smooth rice or vegetable purée to a baby alongside her usual milk feeds. Gradually, as your baby adapts to feeding from a spoon,

the quantity and number of meals can be increased from one mini-meal to three. As she progresses, so the purée can become thicker and coarser, until she can eat a finely chopped version of the family's meal. Solid feeding seems a contradiction in terms, as your baby's first meal will be anything but solid, more like a very thin, smooth porridge or thick cream.

When to start

Most babies are ready to try their first few mini-mouthfuls of solid food between four and six months.

SIGNS THAT YOUR BABY IS READY FOR SOLIDS

♦ She doesn't seem fully satisfied after a feed
♦ She wants feeding more often
♦ She seems generally restless and grizzly
♦ She has begun to wake more often in the night

Occasionally, very large babies may appear to want solid foods earlier than at four months, but this is unusual. Don't be tempted to begin weaning earlier than four months without your doctor's approval, as your baby's digestive system may be too immature to cope and it might also increase the likelihood of allergic reactions. You may also be advised to wait until nearer six months if you have a family history of allergies.

If this is your first baby, you may feel pressurized into offering your child solid foods early on simply because your friends have. Don't yield to such an impulse, it isn't a competition and there are advantages to waiting. Be guided by how you and your baby feel.

In the early days of weaning, the aim is to introduce your baby to the tastes and textures of foods other than milk, not for these new foods to provide lots of extra nourishment.

Sitting comfortably

At first, you and your baby will probably feel happiest if she sits on your lap so that she feels secure. Protect her clothes with a bib or muslin and your own with a tea towel. As feeding progresses and your baby grows, a baby's car seat – placed on a secure surface or the floor – may be easier.

Allow plenty of time so that you and your baby can enjoy this new experience. If you have older children, offer your baby solids when she wakes after a mid-morning sleep, when the other children are at school or playgroup and the house is peaceful. You may prefer to give your baby a small milk feed first so that she isn't frantic, then offer solid foods and a second milk feed to follow.

INTRODUCING SOLIDS

Commercially produced powdered baby rice is probably the easiest first food to offer as it is simple to prepare and the portions required are so small. Mix 1 teaspoon of 'pure' (unsweetened) baby rice to a smooth, slightly sloppy consistency with breast milk, formula milk, or previously boiled and cooled water (see pack instructions). Check the temperature – it should be just lukewarm – then offer this to your baby from a small, rounded, plastic baby spoon. The taste won't be too dissimilar to the milk your baby is used to and should be happily received. If she appears distressed, stop and try again in a few days or weeks' time. Taking food from a spoon is a new skill and can take a while for your baby to learn. Don't worry if more of the food dribbles out than is consumed. At this stage, your baby is learning to chew, rather than just suck, and is still receiving all of her nutritional needs from milk.

If your baby enjoyed the rice, offer it again once a day during the next few days to allow time for her digestive system to adapt, then gradually build up to 2–3 teaspoons of food. Equally, you could offer finely puréed and sieved potato, too. If your baby seems to enjoy these first few mini-mouthfuls, then move on and try some other tastes such as puréed vegetables, fruits or porridge.

Suitable vegetables to purée and sieve as first foods are butternut squash, sweet potato, parsnip or carrot. Peel and dice the vegetable, rinse with water from the kettle, then steam until tender and purée with formula milk, breast milk or boiled water. Alternatively, cook in a little water or formula milk and purée with this liquid. Sieve to make sure it is completely lump-free.

Dessert apples or pears are good fruits to start with. Peel, core and cook diced pear or apple with a little boiled water, but no sugar, purée and sieve.

Try offering a thin porridge of white rice, cornmeal, sago or millet cooked with formula, breast milk or boiled water. (Do not use instant polenta, as the grains have been coated in wheat flour.)

WHAT'S NEXT?

If your baby takes to solids readily, slowly build up to two mini-meals a day over the next four to six weeks, adapting the quantities to suit her appetite. Keep flavours mild and very simple and make sure purées are slightly sloppy, absolutely smooth and lump-free. Maintain milk feeds and aim for 600 ml (1 pint) breast or infant formula milk a day.

WEANING TIPS
♦ Be guided by your baby and health professional.
♦ Learning to eat from a spoon is a tricky skill for a new baby and can be messy.
♦ Never force feed your baby.
♦ Go slowly – try just one new taste at a time in the first few weeks.
♦ Use sterilized equipment up to six months. Continue sterilizing teats and bottles until no longer required (see page 13).

Making your own baby foods

Only the best is good enough for your baby, but that doesn't mean that feeding him need cost the earth or take hours of preparation. In the early days of weaning, it is much easier to batch cook baby foods as amounts are so small and it really doesn't take much longer to purée two carrots rather than one. In addition, making your own baby food ensures that you know exactly what has gone into it and guarantees that it is free from any additives.

BASIC EQUIPMENT
You will probably already have much of the equipment needed for preparing food for your baby. Simply pick and mix the items you already have in your kitchen with a few extras from the suggestions below.

For food preparation
♦ Two small nylon chopping boards, one for fruit and vegetables and one for meat
♦ A small sharp knife
♦ A vegetable peeler

For cooking
♦ A steamer is invaluable and a good way to retain vitamins. If you don't already have a steamer, it is worth investing in a relatively inexpensive, expandable, stainless steel steamer or a larger, but more expensive steamer and saucepan set. Alternatively, improvise with a metal colander set over a medium saucepan and covered with a large lid or foil.
♦ If your saucepans look a little past their best, you may also want to treat yourself to a new, medium, nonstick pan with a lid.

For puréeing
♦ A new, sturdy nylon sieve and a fork or potato masher to press foods through are useful and cheap.

♦ A food mill is an effective, but rather old-fashioned machine that presses foods through a range of discs by means of an easy-to-turn handle. They are simple to assemble and use, come with a range of discs for fine and coarse purées and separate out seeds and skins. They are good for different quantities although they do get a little labour intensive if you are batch cooking large amounts.
♦ A blender saves time and effort and is by far the best way to purée larger amounts of baby food, although they cost a lot more than the above two methods. They blend to a much finer purée than a food processor. If you buy a new one, check it is suitable for blending small quantities without the food getting trapped beneath the blades.
♦ Combination machines are top of the range combinations of food processor and blender. Some even come with smaller spice mills, which are invaluable for finely puréeing tiny quantities of baby food.

For serving food
♦ Look for special plastic baby spoons with small, shallow bowls and soft, rounded edges to avoid harming your baby's gums. Try supermarkets, baby shops and chemists.
♦ To begin with you will need only a tiny china or plastic bowl. As your baby grows and begins to wriggle more, a plastic bowl with a handle will be easier for you to hold on to and save spillage. Larger feeding bowls with nonslip suction bases that adhere to the highchair table are ideal for babies that are keen to feed themselves.

KEEPING SAFE AND CLEAN

♦ Look for spoons and bowls with temperature detectors as these will change colour if the food is too hot to serve to your baby.

♦ To protect your baby's clothes, choose small, soft, fabric bibs or use muslin at first. As your baby grows, move on to plastic backed towelling bibs or wipe clean bibs. For babies who have progressed to feeding themselves, bibs with sleeves can be invaluable. So, too, can plastic bibs with a trough to catch spills.

♦ Highchairs come in a range of designs and prices, from budget clip-on seats that attach directly to the dining table and fold-up highchairs, ideal for small kitchens or when visiting grandparents, to top-of-the-range models with an adjustable seat and tray which can be converted to a small table and chair for later use. Whichever style you choose, make sure that it is sturdy, easy to wipe clean, including the seat (beware of food traps like recessed screw holes), and that the highchair tray or table has raised edges so that food doesn't fall on to the floor. Most importantly, it should have a good harness or harness fixing to keep your child safe and secure at feeding time.

♦ Protect the floor beneath the highchair with a plastic tablecloth, old towel or even sheets of newspaper. This is not so important in the early days of weaning, but essential for older babies keen to feed themselves.

GETTING STARTED

Hygiene is paramount when preparing food for your baby and scares about food poisoning on the television and in the newspapers have made us even more aware of the dangers.

1 Always wash your hands thoroughly before preparing milk feeds and baby food.

2 Wash chopping boards, large utensils and saucepans thoroughly – in a dishwasher, if possible. Alternatively, hand wash items in hot soapy water and rinse with boiling water. Leave to dry on a rack and change tea towels frequently.

3 Sterilize smaller items in a steam sterilizer, a saucepan of boiling water for 5 minutes, or in a cold water solution with sterilizing fluid or tablets, according to the packet instructions, making sure items in water are completely immersed.

4 Continue sterilizing bottles and teats until they are no longer needed and make sure they are clean before going into the sterilizer. Larger items required for food preparation need not be sterilized once your baby is six months old.

5 Keep kitchen work tops scrupulously clean.

6 Use separate bowls, forks and can openers for feeding pets and wash them separately.

Batch cooking

As a baby eats such tiny amounts, especially in the early days of weaning, it can be a great time-saver to make up larger quantities of purée and freeze individual portions for other times. These are ideal to take on outings or to a baby minder or nursery if you return to work. Make a larger quantity of simple purées or double baby recipes, then purée or mash.

Take out a portion for the next meal, cover and chill in refrigerator until needed. Spoon the remainder into sections of a sterilized ice cube tray or mini plastic pots. Cool, loosely covered, then seal and label clearly with the date and type of food. Freeze as soon as possible and use within six weeks. If you are using ice cube trays, open freeze until solid, then pop the cubes into a plastic container, seal and label. (Make sure both trays and containers are sterilized. Use plastic bags from six months). Then take out as many cubes as you require when you need them. As your baby's appetite grows, just increase the number of cubes from one, two, four or more or for new flavour combinations, mix different flavoured cubes together for greater variety.

Thaw mini-dinners overnight in the refrigerator. Heat thoroughly, stirring so that purée doesn't stick to the pan, then cool to the required temperature. Alternatively, microwave for a speedier option, but make sure that the food is defrosted and heated thoroughly and stirred well to dispel any hot spots. Cool for a few minutes, stir again and always check the temperature before serving.

Reheating know-how

When a baby hasn't eaten much, it can be tempting to keep what is left to reheat later. Resist this temptation and always throw leftovers away immediately. Reheating foods more than once provides ideal conditions for bacteria to multiply and for food poisoning to follow.

DON'T FORGET

♦ Always cover just-cooked food and transfer to the refrigerator as soon as possible.
♦ Never reheat food more than once.
♦ If making up a large batch of food, take out one portion for your baby's next meal and chill, then freeze the rest. Do not reheat the whole quantity and then freeze leftovers.
♦ Make sure reheated foods are piping hot, stir well and then leave to cool to the desired temperature.
♦ If using a microwave, leave foods to stand after cooking and always stir well to prevent hotspots.

USING A MICROWAVE

It used to be considered unwise to use a microwave to reheat baby food as it would often heat up unevenly. A microwave oven heats food differently from a conventional oven, with heat spreading from the outside edges towards the centre. To compensate for this, always stir foods well. Allow a few minutes for food to stand and for heat to equalize throughout, then stir again and check the temperature before serving. The other temptation is to heat foods until lukewarm. Although ideal for a baby, this temperature is also perfect for any bacteria present to multiply. To keep food safe, make sure it is piping hot first and then leave to cool to the correct serving temperature.

Getting the texture right

It is essential to get the consistency of your baby's food right. If it is too thick or coarse in the early stages, she will not be able to swallow it. If it is sloppy for too long, she will become a lazy eater who will be reluctant to eat anything that requires much chewing.

By the age of about six months, your baby will begin to learn to chew. If foods are very liquid for too long, this stage of development may be missed and your child may be reluctant to join in family meals later. Be guided by your baby. While it is important that she moves from ultra-smooth purées, first, to mashed and, later, to chopped foods, each child will develop at her own rate and some will take longer than others. Teething brings an additional set of problems. Just like adults, a baby may be reluctant to eat coarser foods if her gums are sore, so wait a few days and then reintroduce coarser foods when she is feeling brighter. As your baby progresses, aim to introduce her to more exciting textures in the same way as you are broadening her experience of different foods.

From 4 months 'easy does it'
Begin with a sloppy, ultra-smooth purée of baby rice or potato. Move on to purées of butternut squash, sweet potato, parsnip or carrot, cooked apple or pear or thin non-gluten porridge.

From 5 months 'more please'
Provide purées with a slightly thicker texture, but make sure they are still smooth. Not all ingredients will need sieving, only those with skins or seeds. Offer new tastes, such as red lentils, avocado and papaya.

From 6–9 months 'lots of new tastes'
At this stage, you can give puréed or mashed mixtures. Progress to coarser textures when your baby is ready to accept them. Offer first finger foods, such as a cooked broccoli or cauliflower floret or cooked carrot stick, at eight or nine months.

From 9–12 months 'I can feed myself'
At this stage, you can give your baby a wide variety of coarsely mashed or chopped meals, plus finger foods, such as cooked or raw vegetables, fruit or toast fingers, to pick up and eat (see page 19).

What's on the menu mum?

The following can be used as a starting point in planning your baby's meals. The information is split into different age groups from 5 months up to 9–12 months for easy access.

FROM 5 MONTHS

If you are introducing solids for the first time at this stage, follow the guidelines on page 11. If your baby is already taking solids, gradually increase their frequency over the next few weeks to three mini-meals daily, spaced as evenly as possible throughout the day. Build on the flavours your baby already enjoys and introduce simple combinations with new flavours too. Be guided by your baby's preferences and don't hurry him. Too many flavours in quick succession may put him off the idea of solids altogether. Aim to increase his repertoire of food gradually and maintain regular milk feeds.

Packed with protein

Sieved red lentils simmered in boiled water and finely mashed or blended with cooked potato, carrot or squash, plus a little vegetable oil may now be introduced. So too can tiny amounts of well-cooked chicken or turkey breast mixed with vegetables. Once your baby has tried and liked a little poultry, try lean and well-cooked lamb or beef mixed with vegetables.

Greater variety

Vegetables with a slightly stronger flavour may now be given. However, it is a good idea to use small quantities to begin with and to mix them with familiar, blander vegetables.

New fruits

You can offer your baby a wider variety of fruit and vegetable fruits, including raw avocado, papaya, banana and melon. Offer new fruits one a time until you know your baby has tried and liked them.

You can then try combining fruits – perhaps a little cooked apple with some banana and melon with pear. Papaya may sound a little exotic for a baby, but once it has been peeled and the black seeds have been removed, it blends to a wonderfully smooth, vibrant orange purée. As it contains the enzyme papain, it is also very easy for a baby to digest.

While many vegetables no longer need sieving, fruits with skins, such as apricots and plums, will still need cooking and sieving before you can serve them to your baby. For a baby who doesn't seem keen on fruit, mix equal quantities of fruit purée and baby rice for a milder, milkier flavour.

Down at the dairy

Tiny portions of easily digestible ricotta cheese, full-fat, mild-tasting yogurt or fromage frais may also be introduced now, although if you have a family history of asthma, eczema or ear problems, you may prefer to wait a month or more.

FOODS TO AVOID Wheat, oats, rye and barley, cow's and goat's milk, hard cheese, nuts and seeds, eggs and fish. Also avoid salt, sugar, honey and offal.

Why avoid grains containing gluten?

Gluten is a protein found in wheat, rye, barley and oats. In some susceptible infants, eating it can lead to the development of coeliac disease whereby the small intestine is damaged. This impairs the absorption of nutrients, causing the child to lose weight. This is highly unlikely to happen, but as it is difficult to detect which babies are susceptible, it is safer to reduce the risks. If this intolerance runs in the family, then the mother will be advised to breastfeed exclusively for up to six months, preferably longer, and to delay the introduction of gluten-containing foods until the baby is at least nine months old.

FROM 6–9 MONTHS

At this stage, most babies will be munching their way through 3 mini-meals a day and weaning foods play a more important nutritional role. Your baby's natural store of iron will now be exhausted, so it is important to include sufficient iron in the diet. A baby's appetite is small and his growth rate high, so it is also vital to provide foods that are a concentrated source of nutrients. Meals may now be thicker smooth purées, moving on to finely mashed or minced meals when your baby is ready.

EACH DAY, AIM TO OFFER:

o 2 mini-portions of fruit and vegetables

o 2 or 3 mini-portions of starchy foods, such as potatoes, rice or unsweetened breakfast cereal

o I mini-serving of protein-rich food, such as cheese, meat, egg, tofu, beans or lentils.

FOODS TO AVOID Nuts, oily fish, shellfish, salt, sugar, honey and offal.

If you have a family history of food allergies or related allergies, such as asthma or eczema, you may be advised to avoid giving your baby dairy products and eggs until much later. Avoid nuts until a child is three years. See also food allergies on page 27.

NEW FOODS

Your baby's digestive system is now more mature and a wider range of foods may be introduced.

♦ Wheat and cereals containing gluten – wheat flour can now be used for sauces. Pasta can be added to baby meals although it will need to be finely chopped or blended.

♦ Full fat cow's milk can now be used, along with mild cheeses, such as cream cheese, mozzarella, Cheddar, Gouda and Edam.

♦ Small quantities of well-cooked, mashed egg yolk or mashed tofu may also be added to baby meals. While amounts of chicken, turkey and lean red meat may be increased and mixed with vegetables, rice or pasta.

♦ Mild-flavoured white fish, such as plaice and sole, and small amounts of trout and salmon may be steamed and added to vegetable or cheese mixtures. It is crucial to check carefully for any bones before cooking and to press the mixture through a sieve afterwards to make sure.

♦ The choice of fruit and vegetables may now be widened to include spinach, cabbage, leek and onion, although it is a good idea to add only small amounts to a food you know your baby already likes as they have such a strong taste. Red, yellow and green peppers may also be used, as well as tiny quantities of skinned and deseeded tomatoes. Again add these in small amounts, as they can be difficult to digest.

♦ You may like to offer a cooked broccoli floret or cooked carrot stick to a baby from eight months. Tiny quantities of soaked, cooked and puréed dried fruits and a little fresh orange juice or puréed and sieved kiwi fruit may also now be included.

♦ Although breast or formula milk feeds are still vitally important, you may find that your baby is happy to lose a lunchtime milk feed. If so, offer him a drink of cooled boiled water instead. Up to the age of eight months, milk is still your baby's main source of protein.

FROM 9–12 MONTHS

By now, your baby may be happy to progress to slightly lumpier food, especially if she has a few milk teeth but, as before, be guided by her. Some hate lumps of any kind and almost seem to gag on them, while others are ready to try lots of new tastes and textures. The most important thing at this stage is to offer variety. If the diet is very limited now, then it can be difficult to encourage children to try new foods later on.

New foods to try

Small portions of well-cooked and mashed frozen peas, dried split peas and chickpeas may now be offered. Providing an allergy is not a consideration, smooth nut and seed butters can be introduced; simply grind lightly toasted hazelnuts, almonds, sunflower or sesame seeds, then blend to a paste with a little vegetable or sunflower oil. The repertoire of fish and meat can be extended by offering small amounts of oily fish. Be extremely vigilant checking for any bones. Canned tuna in water can also be included in the diet, although avoid fish canned in brine as it is too salty. If using small quantities of pulses, you may prefer to use canned beans for convenience; choose a variety without added salt or sugar. Canned tomatoes are also a good store-cupboard ingredient, but use them sparingly as they can be too acidic for young children. Whole eggs may now be used, but make sure they are cooked until the yolk and white are firm.

Eating as a family

Now that your baby is older, you can begin to eat together as a family. Roasts are, perhaps, the easiest to share with some of the vegetables and little of the meat finely chopped or mashed with milk if needed. As it is still important to keep salt out of a baby's diet, season adult portions after she has been served. Stock cubes may be incredibly salty, so make your own salt-free stock with a leftover chicken carcass or make up large batches of vegetable stock and freeze in handy portions. If you are very short of time, use low-salt stock cubes and mix with the double the quantity of water specified.

Babies should still be on a diet free of added sugar, so now is a good time to review how much sugar the rest of the family consumes. Mixing sharper fruits with naturally sweet ones, such as mashed bananas or puréed dates, may soon convert the family.

Most babies will be happy to try more flavourful food, so there is no need to ban garlic or herbs from family meals – simply to cut down the amounts to begin with. Very spicy foods can be off-putting and distressing for a small child, so add these to parent portions once the baby has been served.

If your child hasn't quite mastered a spoon yet, then finger foods can be invaluable. The baby feels part of the group and can happily munch through lots of vegetables while mum and dad are able to eat too.

I CAN FEED MYSELF

Encouraging your baby to feed herself can be a truly messy business. A quite young baby may be surprisingly keen, so offer her an extra spoon to keep little hands busy, allowing you to feed from a second spoon. Cooked broccoli or cauliflower florets or carrot sticks make ideal first finger foods for babies from eight months, as they will withstand a baby's tight grip, but are soft enough not to harm young gums. Once your baby has mastered the tricky art of eye, hand and mouth co-ordination, the fun really starts.

◆ Remember, never leave a child unattended when eating.

OTHER FOODS TO TRY

◆ Peeled banana
◆ Peeled apple slices
◆ Peeled and thickly sliced cucumber
◆ Cubes of mild Cheddar cheese
◆ Buttered toast fingers
◆ Halved rice cakes
◆ Bread sticks
◆ Raisins and sultanas – but don't be alarmed if these seem to pass through whole

Coping with the mess

As your child grows, so does the mess. Protect the floor under the highchair, especially if there is a carpet, with a plastic tablecloth, old towel or sheets of newspaper. Resist the temptation to clean a sticky face and hands until the end of a meal, so that your child can really enjoy the experience of a new and wonderful food. Be on standby with kitchen roll or baby wipes for when she has finished.

FOODS TO AVOID   Blue and unpasteurized cheeses, salt, sugar, honey, peanuts and shellfish.

What to do if a child chokes

◆ Don't waste time trying to remove the food from your baby's mouth unless it can be done quickly.
◆ Turn your baby, head down, supporting her head with your forearm and slap firmly between the shoulder blades.
◆ If this doesn't work, try again.
◆ Don't hesitate to ring your doctor or emergency services if worried.

EACH DAY, AIM TO OFFER:

◆ 3–4 mini-portions of fruit and vegetables
◆ 3–4 mini-portions of starchy foods
◆ 2 mini-portions of protein-rich foods, such as meat, fish, eggs, cheese, lentils and tofu

THE IMPORTANCE OF SNACKS

Once your child is on the move, she can be incredibly active. While her energy and protein requirements are high in relation to her size, her appetite may be very small and it can be difficult to meet these dietary needs from just three main meals a day. Healthy snacks – those not laden with sugar or salt – can make all the difference. Keep snacks small to ensure that your child has room for her main meals. Choose from the following suggestions:

◆ mini fromage frais
◆ diced mild Cheddar cheese
◆ a few bread sticks
◆ half a rice cake
◆ mini sandwiches made with cream cheese and banana, finely grated carrot and cheese
◆ toast fingers
◆ mini hot cross bun, cut into strips
◆ carrot or cucumber sticks
◆ half a banana

What makes a healthy diet?

Although appetites differ, we all need to eat a varied range of different foods, whatever our age. Unlike adults, children need the concentrated energy that fat provides, so it is not advisable to give them low-fat alternatives. A high-fibre diet isn't suitable for young children either because fibre can fill up a tiny tummy before nutritional needs are met. The key to a healthy diet is to make it as interesting and varied as possible, once weaning is well established, and to encourage children to eat a wide range of foods from the four main food groups.

Fruit and vegetables

These are the first foods to offer your baby. They not only add colour and interest to our diet, but are also an essential source of a wide range of vitamins and minerals. Begin

weaning with the milder tasting vegetables, such as potatoes, butternut squash, yams, sweet potatoes, parsnips and carrots, or fruits, such as dessert apples, pears, bananas or papaya. Move on to stronger tasting fruit and vegetables, such as kiwi fruit, red berries, oranges, leafy greens, coloured peppers and sweetcorn.

Protein rich foods

Children grow at such a rate that they need more protein in relation to their body weight than adults. Protein is made up of 20 amino acids, eight of which cannot be manufactured from other proteins in the body. These are essential amino acids and are vital for growth and development. Begin with easy-to-digest, full-fat, soft cheeses,. then move on to red lentils, chicken, turkey, lean red meat and mild tasting fish. Later, introduce eggs, small portions of pulses and finely ground nuts and seeds (but only if there is no history of food allergies).

Grains and cereals

These are needed for energy. When weaning first begins, choose from non-gluten grains, such as ground white rice or long grain white rice, moving on to thin porridge made with sago, millet, maize or tapioca. From six months, grains containing gluten can be offered and these include wheat flour, bread, pasta, oats and barley.

Fats and sugars

Some fat is useful to young children because of the concentrated energy that it provides. Offer it to very young children in the form of easy-to-digest, full-fat, mild tasting cheese or yogurts. Sugars are provided by naturally sweet fruits, such as ripe pears, bananas or dried fruit.

MAXIMIZE THOSE VITAMINS AND MINERALS

♦ As many vitamins and minerals are water soluble, add as little water, formula or breast milk as possible to foods while simmering in a pan and use all the liquid when puréeing.

♦ Don't peel vegetables in advance and leave them in a bowl of cold water until you are ready to cook.

♦ Steam foods for maximum vitamin retention.

♦ Use green leafy vegetables as soon as possible after buying them and keep them out of direct sunlight.

♦ Vitamin C is destroyed by heat and oxidation, so use fruits raw where possible.

♦ Choose fortified breakfast cereals, as they have added vitamins and minerals

Are organic foods best?

Potentially, babies have a greater exposure to chemical residues than most adults. This is because, weight for weight, babies consume far more fruit and vegetables, fruit juices, milk, eggs and other foods that are subject to the pesticides and artificial growth hormones used in intensive farming than adults do. In addition, a child is more liable to absorb residues because his gastrointestinal tract is more easily penetrated.

Fruit and vegetable crops are sprayed with pesticides to prevent plant diseases and to increase the yield. Cows and chickens are given fodder fortified with hormones and antibiotics, traces of which pass into milk and eggs. Increasing consumer awareness of the possible health risks associated with the use of these unnatural substances has led to the demand for organic foods. These are produced without the use of pesticides, growth hormones and additives, so you may prefer to buy them for your baby. As a result of the demand, supermarkets now stock an increasing range of organic fruit and vegetables. Look for organic milk, cheese, eggs and meat too. If you have a local organic farm shop, so much the better as the food should be fresher and less expensive.

What about ready-made baby foods?

Commerical baby foods are convenient, especially if you are out for the day or need to supply a meal for your child at day nursery. For most of your baby's meals, however, homemade foods are the best option – not least because they enable him to get used to the flavours of family meals. Ready-made baby foods also tend to work out much more expensive.

Keep a few cans, jars or dried packs in reserve for emergencies. Dried foods are perhaps the most useful for very young babies whose appetites are so tiny, as you can take out just one or two teaspoons and make up with water, rather than opening a jar and throwing half or more away. Buy gluten-free and dairy-free foods for a baby under six months and choose foods that do not contain added sugars or sweeteners for a baby under one year.

Can I bring up a baby on a vegetarian diet?

It is no longer thought to be cranky or extreme to bring up a baby on a vegetarian diet. In fact, all babies begin with a vegetarian diet for the first month of weaning. Milk, dairy products, eggs and finely ground nuts and seeds (see page 27 for allergies) are all rich in protein, while fruit and vegetables provide valuable sources of vitamins and minerals.

Research has shown that children brought up on a vegetarian diet grow just as well as those who eat meat, provided they are given a mixed diet. While pulses are essential in a vegetarian diet, it is important not to overload a young child with too much fibre, so add only tiny portions of well-cooked red lentils to begin with, moving on to the larger lentils and pulses as your baby approaches his first birthday. Levels of vitamin B12, vitamin D and iron can sometimes be a problem. If you are planning to bring up your baby up on a dairy-free vegetarian diet, talk to your health visitor or doctor for tips and guidelines before you begin weaning.

On the plus side, vegetarians may be less prone to various ailments, such as heart disease, high blood pressure, obesity, diet-related diabetes, gallstones and certain forms of cancer in later life, while being absolutely certain to avoid CJD and E-coli food poisoning.

VITAMIN SUPPLEMENTS

A good, balanced diet should supply all the vitamins and minerals your child needs. However, you may find it reassuring to supplement the diet of a child with a poor appetite or one going through a very fussy stage with specially formulated vitamin drops. Some health authorities recommend vitamin drops for babies over six months and these are available on prescription. If you are at all worried about your child's weight gain, ask a health professional or doctor for advice.

FOODS TO AVOID

Salt

This is too strong for your baby's kidneys, so don't add salt or salty stock cubes when making baby food. Cook baby food in homemade, salt-free chicken or vegetable stock, boiled water, formula or full-fat cow's milk. If your baby is sharing a family meal, add salt to adult portions once his portion has been served. Stock cubes can be used in family meals for babies over nine months, but choose a low-salt brand and make up with extra water. Use concentrated savoury spreads, such as yeast extract, very sparingly and not before your baby is nine months old.

Sugar

Try to avoid adding sugar to baby foods so that you don't bring up your baby with an overly sweet tooth. Sweeten sharper fruits with naturally sweet ones, such as

bananas with plums and ripe pears with a little orange juice. Soak, cook and purée dried apricots or dates and stir into natural yogurt or fromage frais for a delicious dessert. Extremely sharp fruits, such as rhubarb or gooseberries, may require a little sugar to make them palatable, but these are the exceptions. Try to add a sweeter fruit and just the tiniest amount of sugar.

Honey

Do not give honey to a baby under one year old, as it can occasionally cause infant botulism.

Peanuts

Seek advice from a health professional if you have a family history of peanut allergy, and if so, do not offer peanuts in any form to a child under three years old and then only under close supervision. Offer a child without a history of food allergy very finely ground almonds or hazelnuts at nine to 12 months and peanuts from 12 months. Do not give whole nuts to children under five years old.

Offal

Avoid giving large quantities of liver to a child as vitamin A levels are too high. A tiny portion of puréed or finely chopped well-cooked liver may be served to a baby from six to nine months, once a week, until he is over one year.

Shellfish

As incidents of food poisoning with prawns and mussels are high, it is best to avoid giving shellfish to a child under one year old.

Putting it all into practice

Below are some suggested menus to help you put the theory into practice, once weaning is well under way. The tasty three-day menu plans for a baby at 4–6 months, 6–9 months and 9–12 months are displayed in a simple to use, at-a-glance format.

THREE-DAY MENU PLAN FOR A 4–5-MONTH-OLD BABY

	Day 1	Day 2	Day 3
Early morning	Milk feed	Milk feed	Milk feed
Mid-morning	Milk feed and sleep	Milk feed and sleep	Milk feed and sleep
Late breakfast	Puréed banana	Sweet Potato & Apple (see p.32)	Chicken Chowder (see p.35)
Mid-afternoon	Milk feed and sleep	Milk feed and sleep	Milk feed and sleep
Early tea	Sweet Potato & Apple (see p.32)	½ small avocado puréed	Apricot & Millet Fool (see p.36)
Bed	Milk feed	Milk feed	Milk feed

THREE-DAY MENU PLAN FOR A 6–9-MONTH-OLD BABY

	Day 1	Day 2	Day 3
Early morning	Milk feed	Milk feed	Milk feed
Breakfast	Baby cereal	Baby cereal	Baby cereal
Mid-morning	Milk feed and sleep	Milk feed and sleep	Milk feed and sleep
Lunch	Creamed Parsnip & Tofu (see p.39)	Creamy Vegetable Pasta (see p.43)	Baby Cauliflower Cheese (see p.44)
Mid-afternoon	Milk feed and sleep	Milk feed and sleep	Milk feed and sleep
Tea	Carrot & Red Pepper Ambrosia (see p.42) Peach & Apple Fool (see p.48)	Cock-a-leekie Stew (see p.45)	Plaice Florentine (see p.46)
Bed	Milk feed	Milk feed	Milk feed

THREE-DAY MENU PLAN FOR A 9–12-MONTH-OLD BABY

	Day 1	**Day 2**	**Day 3**
Early morning	Milk feed	Milk feed	Milk feed
Breakfast	Baby cereal Apple juice diluted with water	Baby cereal Apple juice diluted with water	Baby cereal Apple juice diluted with water
Mid-morning	Milk feed and sleep	Milk feed and sleep	Milk feed and sleep
Lunch	Mediterranean Veg (see p.52) Mini Apple Custard Pot (see p.62)	Broccoli & Fennel Risotto (see p.54) Remaining ½ papaya, mashed	Moroccan Lamb (see p.56) Prune & Banana Sundae (see p.63)
Mid–afternoon	½ rice cake and water to drink	Fromage frais and water to drink	½ mini hot cross bun, cut into fingers and water to drink
Tea	Mini hummus sandwiches ½ mashed papaya	Eggy Bread Fingers (see p.58) with cucumber and carrot sticks	Tuna Ragu (see p.57) Cubes of ripe pear as finger food
Bed	Milk feed	Milk feed	Milk feed

Coping with a fussy eater

Most children go through a fussy eating stage at some time. It may last a day or two, a week or two or even longer as your child gets older. Some of the most common problems follow and tips on how to cope.

Does your baby spit out more than it eats?

Learning to take food off a spoon can be difficult, especially for a very young baby. It is totally different from the sucking action needed for drinking milk. Try putting less food on the spoon so that your baby's mouth isn't so full. Double check the temperature of the food – is it a little hot or very cold?

Perhaps your baby dislikes the taste. If it's a new flavour, try mixing it with an equal quantity of something he has already tried and liked. Alternatively, if you have just begun weaning, change from baby rice to puréed potato or butternut squash. If that isn't successful, perhaps your baby just isn't ready to go on to solids yet. Wait a week or even two, depending on your child's age, and then try again when you're both feeling relaxed and the house is quiet.

Does your baby seem to have trouble swallowing?

Try thinning the baby food with extra formula or breast milk or a little cooled boiled water. Also try reducing the amount that you put on the spoon. If this doesn't seem to help, then abandon the solid meal and give your baby a milk feed with lots of reassuring cuddles. Try again in a few days time and, if you still have problems, see your health visitor or doctor to check that there is not a more serious reason.

My baby seems to have lost his appetite

Just like an adult's, a baby's appetite can vary enormously from meal to meal and from day to day. It's harder to know why a baby has suddenly stopped eating as he can't explain. Painful gums and sleepless nights while teething are enough to

put anyone off their food. Some babies do not like the change to more textured food, or perhaps your baby is unwilling to try some new flavours. If he refuses food that he has tried and liked before, and the problem persists for several days, check your baby's weight at the clinic and seek advice from your health visitor or doctor.

Meal times are just a battle of wills

As your child gets older, he will quickly realize that refusing food provokes a reaction from you, especially if you're tired and have other children at the table. Try to stay calm and explain quietly that if he doesn't want any dinner, that's fine, but there won't be biscuits, crisps or sweets instead. If he is very hungry later on, offer a piece of fruit or a mini-pot of fromage frais or bring the next meal forward a little. Making a child sit at table until everything has been eaten just becomes a power struggle with tears of frustration on both sides.

Try not to fall into the trap of serving only food that you know your child will eat, as this can quickly lead to your having to cook two meals each time – one for the fussy toddler and something else for the rest of the family. Alternate meal types. Offer a chicken nuggets or fishfinger style supper one night, a meaty casserole the next and then pasta, with vegetables you know your child likes plus some others for variety. If you feel really fed up, try a picnic to take the pressure off everyone.

DON'T DESPAIR

♦ Never force a baby to have the last teaspoon in the bowl. He will soon turn his head away when he's had enough.

♦ No baby will starve himself. Continue offering a variety of foods and don't despair; the food fad will disappear just as quickly as it arrived.

♦ Talk over any worries with your health professional or doctor.

Food allergies

Some children are more susceptible to an allergic reaction triggered by a particular food. Those most at risk are from families with a history of an allergy, such as nut allergy, asthma, eczema and/or hay fever. An estimated one in ten children is prone to allergy. Although many grow out of their allergies by the time they are two, others will have a sensitivity to nuts, eggs, milk or shellfish for life. The Department of Health recommends that infants who have a strong family history of allergy should be breastfed for at least four months, longer if possible. Weaning should be delayed until five or six months and new foods introduced one at a time. Seek expert advice before modifying a child's diet or if you feel that there may be something wrong with your baby.

FOODS MOST LIKELY TO CAUSE ALLERGIES

Peanuts and other nuts

Peanuts can cause anaphylactic shock, a particularly severe allergic reaction where the throat swells and breathing gets difficult. Those who are prone must take great care to avoid peanuts, peanut butter and unrefined peanut oil, particularly in ready-meals and snacks. Always read food labels carefully.

Do not include peanuts in a baby's diet if there is a family history of hay fever, asthma or eczema and introduce them carefully and under close supervision when your child is over three years old. It is rare to be allergic to other nuts, such as hazelnuts, walnuts or almonds, but seek advice from your local doctor about the introduction of these in your child's diet.

Dairy products

Some children lack lactase – the enzyme needed to digest milk sugar. Tummy aches and diarrhoea are possible indications, so consult your doctor if worried. Affected children may need to limit or omit cow's milk, cheese and butter from their diet.

Soya milk and other soya products are suitable substitutes. Yogurt may be tolerated, as the bacteria in it produce their own lactase. Some babies may also be allergic to cow's milk protein (and soya-based milks too) and will require a hypoallergenic milk formula available on prescription.

Gluten

Gluten is found in wheat, barley, rye and oats, as well as wheat-based products, such as bread and pasta. If there is a family history of coeliac disease, it is important to delay the introduction of oats, rye and barley until your baby is nine months old and wheat until your baby is over 12 months.

Babies with gluten intolerance may suffer from diarrhoea and tummy problems, causing damage to the intestine lining and weight loss. If diagnosed, choose rice cakes for bread, rice or corn noodles for wheat pasta, and buy rice or corn (maize) cereals for breakfast. Also use buckwheat, millet and sorghum.

Eggs

These can cause problems with a number of children. Rashes, swelling and tummy upsets are possible indicators.

Tomatoes

These may cause eczema in young children. If your family has a history of allergies, don't include in your child's diet until nine months old. They may also be associated with hyperactivity.

Citrus fruit and strawberries

A reaction to these may bring your baby out in a rash. If she has had an allergic reaction, don't re-introduce these fruits until your baby is over 12 months.

Complete baby food guide

This invaluable guide will help you to see what foods to introduce to your baby and when. Not all babies are ready to start on solid foods at exactly four months, so use the age groups as a rough guide. If your baby starts weaning later, then introduce foods from the second group – 5–6 months – between four and eight weeks after weaning has commenced. Aim to have your baby following a mixed diet with plenty of texture by the time he is 11–12 months.

4 MONTHS

Texture	Ultra-smooth, slightly sloppy sieved purée
Flavours	Offer just one mild flavour at a time for 3–4 meals
Solid meals per day	Tiny portions of 1–3 teaspoons, once a day to begin with, moving on to 2 mini-meals
Vegetables	Cooked potato, sweet potato, butternut squash, parsnip, carrot
Fruit	Peeled and cored dessert apples or pears cooked with a little boiled water but no sugar, then puréed and sieved
Grains and pulses	Non-gluten grains: baby rice, plain white rice, cornmeal/polenta (only if grains are not coated in wheat flour), sago, millet or tapioca cooked to a thin porridge and sieved if needed
Dairy foods	No
Nuts & seeds	No
Meat	No
Fish	No
Milk	Usual breastfeeds or at least 600 ml (1 pint) infant formula milk

5 MONTHS

Texture	Smooth, slightly thicker purées, not necessarily sieved
Flavours	Offer one new mild flavour at a time
Solid meals per day	2–3
Vegetables	Cooked and puréed courgette with the skin on, cauliflower, broccoli
Fruit	Puréed raw papaya, banana, melon, mango; avocado, cooked apricots and ripe plums, without sugar and sieved to remove the skins
Grains and pulses	Tiny portions of well-cooked red lentils puréed with vegetables and a few drops of vegetable oil
Dairy foods	Tiny portions of ricotta cheese, full-fat yogurt, fromage frais *
Nuts & seeds	No
Meat	Tiny portions of well-cooked chicken or turkey mixed with vegetables, moving on to lean red meat
Fish	No
Milk	Usual breastfeeds or a minimum of 600 ml (1 pint) infant formula milk

* **see page 27 for details on food allergies**

6–9 MONTHS

Texture	Thicker, smooth purée or very finely mashed or minced foods
Flavours	Simple blends of foods your baby likes with new foods for a more varied diet
Solid meals per day	3 – first finger foods, such as cooked broccoli and carrot can be introduced from 8 months
Vegetables	Stronger tasting vegetables, such as spinach, cabbage, leek, onion, sweetcorn, celery, fennel and peppers*, plus tiny amounts of fresh skinned, deseeded tomato*
Fruit	Tiny amounts of cooked, puréed dried fruits, skinned, puréed kiwi, freshly squeezed orange juice*
Grains and pulses	Wheat and other gluten cereals, such as pasta, barley, oats and plain flour in sauces. Small portions of quinoa, well-mashed beans and larger lentils
Dairy foods	Full fat cow's milk in cooking, but not as a drink, mild tasting cheeses – Cheddar, Edam, Gouda, mozzarella, cream cheese; hardboiled and mashed egg yolk,* small amounts of tofu
Nuts & seeds	No
Meat	Increase range of lean meat
Fish	Steamed plaice, sole, trout, small amounts of salmon. Flake carefully, making certain there are no bones. Sieve if needed. Mix with vegetable purée
Milk	Usual breastfeeds or at least 500–600 ml (17 fl oz —1 pint) infant formula or follow-on milk

9–12 MONTHS

Texture	Coarsely mashed blends and finger foods – toast strips, fresh fruit, vegetables
Flavours	Can now offer mashed portions of family meals, providing no salt or sugar has been added
Solid meals per day	3, plus 1 or 2 healthy snacks
Vegetables	Wide range of vegetables; you can now give peas, aubergines, canned tomatoes
Fruit	Unsweetened fruit juices as a drink, diluted 1 part to 10 parts with water. Canned fruit in natural juice. Sieved strawberries, raspberries, red and blackcurrants. Sharper fruits, such as rhubarb and gooseberries, mixed with tiny amounts of sugar
Grains and pulses	A wider range of grains, but limit unrefined grains. Introduce cooked dried peas in casseroles and homemade hummus; couscous for added texture
Dairy foods	Increase amounts and variety; avoid blue or unpasteurized cheeses. Can use butter or margarine; well-cooked and mashed whole eggs
Nuts & seeds	Finely ground nuts and seeds mixed to a paste, spread over toast; add to casseroles*
Meat	Gradually increase amounts and offer a wider variety, including tiny amounts of ham
Fish	Tiny portions of oily fish mixed with vegetables, wider variety of white fish, but be very careful to remove all bones. Canned tuna in water. Avoid strongly flavoured smoked fish, such as kippers, and shellfish until your baby is over 12 months old
Milk	Usual breastfeeds night and morning or 500–600 ml (17 fl oz —1 pint) formula milk or follow-on milk as 6–9 months

FROM 4 MONTHS

The introduction of those first few mini-mouthfuls of baby purée is an exciting time for both mother and baby. For your baby's first meal, keep the serving minute and think of it more as a taster sample than a real meal. If your baby is happy to accept food from a spoon, offer a teaspoon or two to begin with at just one meal a day.

After a week or so, introduce a second baby meal, but again keep portions small so that your baby's digestive system is not overloaded. Flavours should be very bland at this stage while your baby makes the transition from milk to solids. Babies don't mind repetition, so offer baby rice for 3–4 meals in a row, then try potato, again for several meals in a row, or alternate with rice. After two or three weeks, try butternut squash, apple or pear purée and then move on to parsnip or carrot purée. At this stage, you are really just trying to get your baby to accept the idea of a meal from a spoon, while her nourishment is still coming primarily from milk.

Rice purée

**2 PORTIONS
(4 MONTHS)**

While baby rice, which comes as a fine rice powder, is a great convenience food, you may like to make your own.

TIPS

♦ Cleanliness is vitally important, so sterilize bowls and spoons in the same way that you do bottles. Wash larger items in the dishwasher or hand wash and sterilize by boiling in water for 3 minutes. See page 13 for extra information.

♦ Don't be tempted to add salt or sugar as your baby's immature digestive system can't yet cope.

150 ml (¼ pint) water
1 tablespoon risotto, basmati or long grain white rice
1–2 tablespoons breast or formula milk

1 Bring the water to the boil in a small pan. Put the rice into a sieve, wash it with cooled boiled water, then drain and add to the pan. Bring back to the boil and simmer for 12–15 minutes, until the rice is tender. Purée in a blender with the milk until a sloppy purée, then press through a sieve. Divide the purée between two bowls, depending on your baby's appetite.

2 Serve one portion. Cover and chill the remaining purée. Use the second portion within 24 hours. Mix it with a little extra warm formula milk or just boiled water to soften the rice to the desired texture. Test the temperature before serving.

Potato purée

This may seem dull, but don't forget your baby's diet has been just milk for the last four months. Don't be tempted to add flavourings or seasonings.

TIP

♦ Make sure that the heat is low or the milk will catch on the base of the pan.

150 g (5 oz) potato, peeled and diced
150 ml (¼ pint) formula milk or water

1 Put the potato into a sieve, rinse with boiling water, then drain and put into a small pan. Add two-thirds of the milk or water, bring to the boil, cover and simmer for 10 minutes, until the potato is tender. Check once or twice during cooking to ensure it hasn't boiled dry.

2 Spoon the mixture into a blender and mix briefly until a smooth, slightly sloppy purée, gradually adding in the remaining milk or water. Press through a sieve.

3 Divide the purée between two bowls. Serve one portion immediately. Cover and chill the remainder and use within 24 hours. Soften with extra warmed formula milk or just boiled water.

Apple purée

**2 PORTIONS
(4 MONTHS)**

Use sweet, mild apples like Gala and mix with baby rice for a milder taste.

TIP

♦ Pear purée can be made in exactly the same way as apple and also freezes well. Choose a ripe pear for maximum flavour and natural sweetness.

1 dessert apple, quartered, cored and peeled
1 tablespoon boiled water

1 Dice the apple, put it into a sieve, rinse with cooled boiled water and drain. Put the apple into a small pan with the water, cover and simmer gently for 10 minutes, checking from time to time. Purée in a blender, then sieve or simply press through a sieve, adding a little extra cooled boiled water if necessary.

2 Serve one portion immediately. Cover the rest and store in the refrigerator. Use within 24 hours.

Butternut squash purée

Butternut squash makes the most wonderful, fine, vibrant orange purée and is an ideal vegetable to freeze.

TIPS

♦ For a bright green alternative, cook and purée diced courgette in the same way. Sieve the purée for young babies.

♦ The larger the dice, the longer they will take to cook.

250 g (8 oz) butternut squash, peeled and deseeded
6 tablespoons formula milk

1 Dice flesh of the squash, put it into a sieve, rinse with boiled water and drain. Place the squash in the top of a steamer, cover and cook over a pan of boiling water for 10 minutes, until tender. Transfer to a blender and purée, gradually adding the milk until a smooth purée forms. Sieve if necessary.

2 Spoon a portion into a bowl and serve. Cover and chill the remainder, then freeze in sections of an ice cube tray.

Parsnip purée

**3–4 PORTIONS
(4–5 MONTHS)**

With its delicate sweetness, parsnip is a good vegetable for a baby who is not keen on solid foods.

TIP

♦ Carrots may also be cooked in the same way. Mix them with a little cooked potato when you first introduce them to your baby.

150 ml (¼ pint) water
250 g (8 oz) parsnips, peeled and diced
5–6 tablespoons formula milk

1 Pour the water into a small pan and bring to the boil. Meanwhile, put the parsnips in a sieve and rinse with boiled water. Add them to the pan, cover and simmer for 15 minutes, until tender. Spoon the parsnips and any remaining cooking water into a blender and process until smooth, gradually adding milk as needed.

2 Spoon one portion into a bowl and serve. Cover and chill the remainder, then freeze in an ice cube tray.

Now that weaning is underway and your baby is happy and keen to take food off a spoon, new foods can be introduced. Try not to hurry her at this stage and follow her lead. You may find the best and most successful way to introduce a new food is to mix it with one that your baby has already tried and liked.

Broccoli & potato

**2–3 PORTIONS
(5–6 MONTHS)**

This mild first taste of green vegetables is a good source of folic acid and vitamin C.

TIPS

♦ If you have a very powerful blender, you may not need to sieve the purée.

♦ As your baby grows, reduce the liquid slightly to make a thicker purée.

125 g (4 oz) potato, peeled and diced
200–250 ml (7–8 fl oz) formula milk or boiled water
75 g (3 oz) broccoli, cut into small florets, stems sliced

1 Rinse the potato with cooled boiled water, drain and put into a small pan with 150 ml (¼ pint) of the milk or water. Cover and simmer for 10 minutes. Add the broccoli, cover and cook for 5 more minutes, until the vegetables are just tender. Purée in a blender, gradually adding the remaining milk or water, then press through a sieve if required.

2 Serve one portion immediately. Cover and chill the remainder, then freeze in an ice cube tray.

Sweet potato & apple:

Make a similar puree by boiling 1 sweet potato, about 200 g (7 oz), peeled and diced and 1 sweet dessert apple, peeled, cored and diced in 175–200 ml (6–7 fl oz) formula milk or boiled water. Cover and simmer for 12–15 minutes, until the sweet potato is tender. Process the mixture in a blender with the remaining milk or water, then press through a sieve. Serve one portion immediately. Cover and chill the remainder, then freeze in an ice cube tray.

Chicken chowder

**2–3 PORTIONS
(5–6 MONTHS)**

Packed with
protein, this
creamy smooth
purée has just
a hint of
chicken flavour.

TIPS

◆   If the chicken is
simmered over a very low
heat, you will probably not
need to add the extra milk or
water when puréeing.

◆   As weaning becomes
more established, you will be
able to stop sieving foods, but
do make sure purées are still
smooth at this stage.

125 g (4 oz) potato, peeled and diced
50 g (2 oz) carrot, peeled and diced
50 g (2 oz) skinless, boneless chicken breast, diced
150–200 ml (5–7 fl oz) formula milk or boiled water

1 Rinse the potato, carrot and chicken with cooled
boiled water. Drain and put into a small pan with
the 150 ml (¼ pint) of the milk or water. Cover and
simmer for 15 minutes, until vegetables are tender
and the chicken is thoroughly cooked. Process in a
blender. Gradually add the remaining milk or water,
if necessary to make a smooth purée, then press
through a sieve.

2 Serve one portion. Cover and chill the remainder,
then freeze in an ice cube tray.

Apple & pear duet

TIP

♦ Choose ripe pears and mild tasting gala apples for maximum natural sweetness

1 sweet dessert apple
1 ripe pear
3 tablespoons boiled water

1 Peel, core and roughly chop the apple and pear. Put the fruit and water into a small pan, cover and simmer for 10 minutes, until the fruit is very soft, then press through a sieve.

2 Serve one portion immediately. Cover and cool the remainder, then freeze in an ice cube tray.

Apricot & millet fool

2–3 PORTIONS
(5–6 MONTHS)

TIP

♦ If you can't buy fresh apricots, use ripe, sweet-tasting plums or fresh peaches instead.

2 tablespoons millet flakes
3 small apricots, well washed, pitted and chopped
about 200 ml (7 fl oz) formula milk or water

1 Put all of the ingredients into a small saucepan and bring to the boil over a low heat. Cook, stirring constantly, for 4–5 minutes, until thickened and the apricots are soft. Process in a blender, then press through a sieve to remove the apricot skins.

2 Serve one portion immediately. Cover and cool the remainder, then freeze in an ice cube tray. As the mixture thickens on cooling, you may need to thin it with a little extra milk or water before serving.

Get Fresh

From five months you can begin to offer your baby fresh fruit purées. Packed with vitamins and minerals and made in minutes, these are ideal convenience foods for babies. For his first taste it may be better to mix the fruit purée with a little made-up baby rice or homemade rice purée so that the flavour isn't quite so pronounced.

PAPAYA & MELON

Papaya (sometimes called paw-paw) has a slightly perfumed flavour and is easy for babies to digest. Babies like the mild flavour of melon. Begin with ogen or honeydew, then move on to orange-fleshed melons such as cantaloupe and charentais: these contain more vitamin C and beta carotene, the plant form of vitamin A.

Halve or wedge a ripe papaya or melon and scoop out and discard any seeds. Scoop the flesh from the skin and process until smooth in a blender – there is no need to sieve. Use one portion immediately and freeze the remainder in sections of an ice cube tray.

BANANA

As bananas ripen the starch changes to sugars, which not only makes them taste better, but also means they are easier for your baby to digest.

Peel and mash half a banana with a fork. Sieve and mix in 1–2 teaspoons formula or breast milk to make a smooth purée. Do not freeze. Make the purée just before you need it, as banana quickly discolours.

AVOCADO

Avocado has the highest protein content of all fruit, and is rich in vitamin E and potassium. Its high levels of monounsaturated fatty acids are a good energy source.

Sieve the flesh of half a small ripe avocado. Add 2–3 teaspoons formula milk or cooled boiled water to make a smooth purée. Do not freeze and use at once.

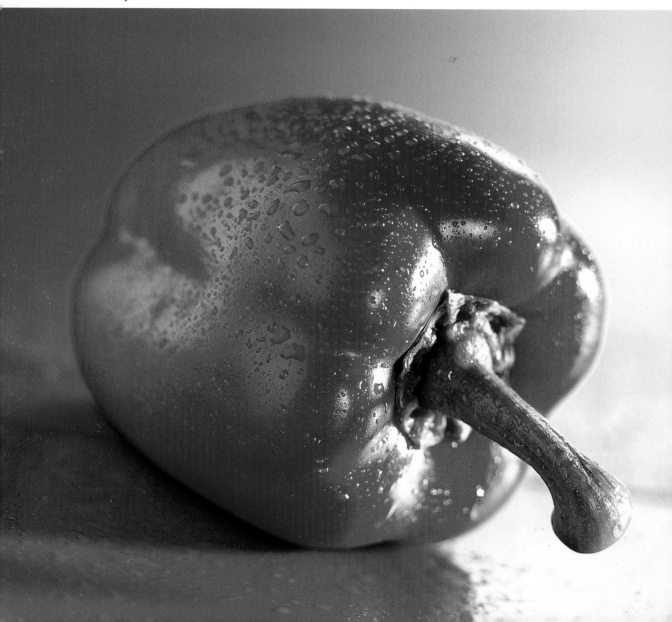

Creamed parsnip & tofu

**2 PORTIONS
(6–9 MONTHS)**

Blended with mashed parsnip, tofu takes on a mild creaminess and makes a simple supper that is packed with protein. If you give your baby small amounts of tofu early on – she is more likely to be receptive than if she first tastes it as an older child.

TIPS

♦ Tofu is one of the few sources of plant protein that supplies all of the essential amino acids.

♦ The small amount of fresh orange juice aids the absorption of calcium from parsnips and iron from tofu.

♦ As the purée is very slightly sweet, it is a good meal with which to tempt a baby who seems to have lost her appetite.

2 small parsnips, about 300 g (10 oz), peeled, diced
    and rinsed
50 g (2 oz) tofu, drained and crumbled
1 tablespoon fresh orange juice
100–150 ml (3½ fl oz–¼ pint) full-fat milk

1 Put the parsnips in the top of a steamer, cover and cook over boiling water for 10 minutes, until just soft.

2 Transfer the parsnips to a blender or food processor and add the tofu and orange juice. Mix until smooth, gradually adding in enough milk to make a smooth, thick purée. Adjust the thickness as your baby matures.

3 Serve half immediately. Cover and chill the remainder and use within 24 hours or freeze for another meal. Add a little extra water or milk before serving if needed.

Baby spinach dhal

**2 PORTIONS
(6–9 MONTHS)**

Attractively
speckled with
finely chopped
spinach, this
dhal is mildly
spiced to suit
very young
tastebuds. Red
lentils are less
fibrous than
other varieties,
so they are a
good way to
introduce a
little fibre
into your baby's
diet.

TIPS

♦ Lentils and rice supply all
the essential amino acids
your baby needs in one meal.

♦ Adding tomato at the end
of cooking boosts vitamin C
levels, helping to maximize
the absorption of calcium
and iron from the lentils
and spinach.

♦ Make up a batch of your
own homemade salt-free
vegetable stock and freeze
in an ice cube tray.

40 g (1½ oz) red lentils, rinsed
25 g (1 oz) long grain white rice
1 teaspoon sunflower oil
pinch of ground coriander
pinch of ground turmeric
250 ml (8 fl oz) homemade vegetable stock or water
25 g (1 oz) frozen chopped spinach, thawed, or
      fresh trimmed spinach
1 fresh tomato, skinned, deseeded and finely chopped

1 Put the lentils, rice, oil, spices and stock or water
into a saucepan and bring to the boil. Cover and
simmer, stirring occasionally, for 25 minutes, or until
the lentils are soft. Top up with extra water or stock
if needed.

2 Stir in the spinach and chopped tomato and cook
for 2 minutes. Process to a smooth thick purée,
adjusting the texture as your baby matures.

3 Serve half immediately. Cover and chill the
remainder, using it within 24 hours.

Askew Road Library

Pumpkin pilaf

**2 PORTIONS
(6–9 MONTHS)**

For this baby pilaf, millet grains take the place of the more traditional rice. They are cooked with pumpkin and lightly flavoured with allspice. When pumpkins are out of season, you can substitute with butternut squash.

TIPS

♦ A gluten-free cereal, millet provides a good source of energy, protein, B vitamins and minerals. This grain also contains silicon, needed for healthy bones, teeth, nails and hair. Millet is available as whole grains that are used like rice or couscous, and as flakes to make porridge.

♦ As you would expect from the vivid colour of pumpkin flesh, it is a good source of beta-carotene, which the body converts to vitamin A; it also provides vitamin E. Pumpkin is easily digested and therefore makes an ideal food for young babies.

40 g (1½ oz) millet grain, rinsed
125 g (4 oz) pumpkin, peeled, deseeded and diced
1 tablespoon raisins (optional)
pinch of ground allspice
1 small bay leaf
300 ml (½ pint) homemade vegetable stock or water

1 Put all of the ingredients into a saucepan and bring to the boil. Cover and simmer for 20–25 minutes, until the millet is soft. Top up with extra stock or water as needed. Discard the bay leaf and mix in a blender or food processor to a smooth thick purée, adjusting the texture as your baby matures.

2 Serve half immediately. Cover and chill the remainder and use within 24 hours or freeze for another meal.

Carrot & red pepper ambrosia

**2 PORTIONS
(6–9 MONTHS)**

Quick and easy
to make, this
brightly
coloured purée
is bound to
attract your
baby's
attention.

TIPS

◆ The more vibrant a
vegetable is, the more
beta-carotene present. Our
bodies convert beta-carotene
into vitamin A, which is
essential for eye function,
immunity, growth and cell
maintenance.

◆ White rice is low in fibre,
so it is an ideal weaning food.
Don't be tempted to introduce
brown rice yet – your baby's
digestive system is still
relatively immature and
unable to cope with a high
fibre intake.

1 carrot, about 125 g (4 oz), peeled and finely diced
¼ red pepper, cored, deseeded and finely chopped
25 g (1 oz) risotto rice, rinsed
200 ml (7 fl oz) homemade vegetable stock or water
1 fresh rosemary sprig (optional)
2–3 tablespoons full-fat milk

1 Put the carrot, red pepper, rice and stock or water
into a saucepan. Add the rosemary, if using. Bring
to the boil, partially cover the pan and simmer for
15 minutes, or until the rice is tender and most of the
liquid has been absorbed. Discard the rosemary.

2 Process the vegetables and rice with enough milk
to make a smooth, thick purée, adjusting the texture
as your baby matures.

3 Serve half immediately. Cover and chill the
remainder and use within 24 hours or freeze for
another meal. Add a little extra water or milk before
reheating if needed.

Creamy vegetable pasta

**2 PORTIONS
(6–9 MONTHS)**

Once you can
begin to cook
pasta for your
baby, it won't
seem long
before she is
joining in all
family meals.
Here, broccoli
and green
beans boost
nutrient levels
and cream
cheese melts to
make a creamy
sauce.

TIP

♦ Broccoli is one of the few
vegetables liked by most
children. Rich in vitamin C,
it is also a useful source of
beta-carotene, folate, iron and
potassium. It also contains
beneficial phytochemicals
that may help to protect
against cancer.

40 g (1½ oz) tagliatelle, macaroni or small pasta shapes
50 g (2 oz) broccoli, cut into small florets
25 g (1 oz) green beans, sliced
3 tablespoons full-fat cream cheese
a few fresh basil leaves (optional)
3–5 tablespoons full-fat milk

1 Cook the pasta in a pan of boiling water for
6–8 minutes, or until tender. Meanwhile, steam the
broccoli florets and green beans over boiling water for
5 minutes until tender.

2 Drain the cooked pasta and place in a blender or
food processor with the vegetables, cream cheese
and basil, if using. Process, adding enough milk to make a
smooth purée.

3 Serve half immediately. Cover and chill the
remainder and use within 24 hours or freeze for
another meal.

Baby cauliflower cheese

**2 PORTIONS
(6–9 MONTHS)**

You don't need
to prepare a
cheese sauce
for your baby,
simply purée all
the ingredients
together for a
deliciously mild,
quick-to-make,
cheesy supper.

TIP

♦   Adding milk and cheese
to baby meals is a good way
to include plenty of protein
and calcium in the diet,
especially if your baby doesn't
seem to be drinking as much
milk. A 40 g (1½ oz) portion
of Cheddar cheese is
equivalent to 200 ml (7 fl oz)
of milk.

1 small potato, about 150 g (5 oz), peeled, diced
        and rinsed
150 g (5 oz) cauliflower, cut into small florets
2.5 cm (1 inch) piece leek, well rinsed and thinly sliced
40 g (1½ oz) mild Cheddar cheese, grated
75–125 ml (3–4 fl oz) full-fat milk

1 Put the potato in a steamer over boiling water,
cover and cook for 10 minutes. Add the cauliflower
and leek and cook for a further 5 minutes, until all the
vegetables are just tender.

2 Transfer the steamed vegetables to a blender or
food processor, add the cheese and process,
gradually adding enough milk to make a smooth, thick
purée. (For older babies you are unlikely to need all
the milk.) Alternatively mash the ingredients together,
making sure there are no lumps at this stage.

3 Serve half immediately. Cover and chill the
remainder and use within 24 hours or freeze for
another meal.

Cock-a-leekie stew

**3 PORTIONS
(6–9 MONTHS)**

As your baby
grows and
enjoys solid
foods, you can
begin to include
foods with a
little more
flavour. Dried
herbs have
been used
here, but a few
sprigs of fresh
herbs from the
garden could
also be used,
if available.

TIPS

♦   Breastfed babies are
often more receptive to
meals with more flavour, as
breast milk changes slightly
depending on what foods the
mother has been eating.

♦   Homemade, salt-free
chicken stock may be added
instead of water, but do not
use stock cubes. Even low-salt
varieties have too much salt
and concentrated flavourings
for a baby of this age.

♦   As your baby grows and
has more teeth, adjust the
texture, gradually changing
from a smooth, thick purée
to a mashed and later, a finely
chopped mixture.

2.5 cm (1 inch) piece of green leek, halved
200 g (7 oz) potato, peeled and diced
125 g (4 oz) boneless, skinless chicken breast, diced
75 g (3 oz) carrot, peeled and diced
1 ready-to-eat pitted prune, quartered
pinch mixed dried herbs
200 ml (7 fl oz) boiled water

1 Wash the leek well under cold running water, drain
and thinly slice. Put the potato, chicken and carrot
into a sieve, rinse with cold water, drain well and put
into a small pan with the leek, prune and herbs. Pour in
the water, bring to the boil, then cover and simmer
gently for 20 minutes.

2 Spoon the vegetables, chicken, prune and half the
cooking liquid into a blender or food processer and
process to the desired texture, gradually adding the
remaining liquid, as required. Serve one portion
immediately. Cover and chill the remainder, then spoon
into sections of an ice cube tray and freeze.

Plaice florentine

**3 PORTIONS
(6–9 MONTHS)**

Plaice has such a delicate flavour that it is sure to win round even the most reluctant of fish eaters.

TIPS

♦ The mascarpone adds a wonderful creaminess to the sauce, but you could also use full-fat cream cheese, ricotta, cottage or grated Cheddar cheese instead.

♦ Pink trout fillets are also delicious cooked in this way. As with all fish cookery, check carefully for bones and sieve the fish to make sure.

♦ Serve a fruit purée for dessert so that the vitamin C in the fruit will aid the absorption of the iron present in the watercress.

1 small fillet of plaice, rinsed
200 g (7 oz) potato, peeled and diced
200 ml (7 fl oz) full-fat milk
125 g (4 oz) courgette, trimmed and diced
3 watercress sprigs
1 tablespoon mascarpone cheese

1 Cook the fish, covered in a steamer for 5 minutes, or until fish is opaque and flakes easily. Remove from the steamer and flake, carefully checking for bones.

2 Meanwhile, simmer the potato and milk in a covered small saucepan for 5 minutes. Add the courgette and cook for 3 minutes. Add the watercress and cook for 2 more minutes. Drain, reserving the milk.

3 Put the fish into a blender with the vegetables, mascarpone and half the milk. Process to the desired texture, gradually adding the milk, as needed.

4 Serve one portion immediately. Cover and chill remainder, then freeze in an ice cube tray.

Plum & ricotta purée

2–3 PORTIONS (6–9 MONTHS)

Plums are puréed and mixed with creamy Italian ricotta cheese to make a nutritious dessert. For optimum sweetness, prepare in quantity when fresh plums are plentiful and ripe and freeze portions for future use.

TIPS

♦ Plums contain vitamin E, an antioxidant that helps to protect cells from damage. They are also a good source of potassium.

♦ Combining plums with soft cheese boosts protein and calcium levels.

2 large ripe plums, about 200 g (7 oz), washed, pitted and roughly chopped
1 tablespoon water
pinch of ground cinnamon (optional)
3 tablespoons ricotta cheese

1 Put the plums in a small saucepan with the water and the cinnamon, if using. Cover and cook gently for 5 minutes, until soft. Remove from the heat and leave to cool.

2 Spoon the plums and ricotta into a blender or food processor and process until smooth. Press through a sieve to remove the skins.

3 Serve a third or half immediately. Cover and chill the remainder and use within 24 hours or freeze for another meal.

Peach & apple fool

**2 PORTIONS
(6–9 MONTHS)**

This creamy, smooth fruit fool is naturally sweet, with just a hint of cardamom. Adults and older children can enjoy it as a sauce spooned over sliced peaches and ice cream. For optimum flavour, use ripe peaches and naturally sweet dessert apples.

TIPS

♦   Rich in vitamin C, this dessert will boost the absorption of iron if it follows an iron-rich main course.

♦   Some bought fruit yogurts contain a surprising amount of sugar. By making your own desserts, it's easy to omit sugar and ensure your baby's food is free from additives.

1 peach, rinsed, halved, pitted and roughly chopped
1 dessert apple, rinsed, quartered, cored and roughly chopped
1 tablespoon water
2 cardamom pods, bruised (optional)
2 tablespoons natural bio yogurt

1 Put the peach and apple into a small saucepan with the water and the cardamom pods, if using. Cover and simmer gently for 5 minutes, until the fruit is tender. Remove the cardamom pods and discard.

2 Purée the fruit in a blender or food processor until smooth, then press through a sieve to remove the fruit skins and cardamom seeds. Cover and leave to cool, then mix the purée with the yogurt.

3 Serve half immediately. Cover and chill the remainder and use within 24 hours or freeze for another meal.

Mixed vegetable platter

**2 PORTIONS
(9–12 MONTHS)**

Mild-tasting
sunflower seed
paste gives this
vegetarian feast
a protein boost.
Vary the mix of
vegetables; red
peppers, green
beans, parsnips,
courgettes and
spinach all work.

TIPS

♦ Sunflower seeds contain
protein, B group vitamins and
calcium.

♦ If possible, buy organically
grown vegetables for your
family's meals.

♦ Alternatively you could
use fortified soya milk instead
of full-fat cow's milk.

1 small potato, about 125 g (4 oz), peeled and diced
1 small carrot, about 125 g (4 oz), peeled and diced
125 g (4 oz) butternut squash, peeled and diced
50 g (2 oz) broccoli, cut into small florets, stems sliced
4 teaspoons sunflower seeds
1 teaspoon sunflower oil
2–3 tablespoons full-fat milk

1 Rinse the potato, carrot and squash, drain and put
into a steamer set over a saucepan of simmering
water. Cover and steam for 10 minutes. Add the
broccoli, cover the pan again and cook for a further
5 minutes.

2 Meanwhile, grind the sunflower seeds to a smooth
paste with the oil and 1 tablespoon of the milk in a
food processor spice mill attachment or a well-washed
coffee grinder. Alternatively, pound the seeds using a
pestle and mortar, gradually adding the oil and milk.

3 Mash or chop the vegetables, mixing in the
sunflower seed paste and enough milk to give
the required consistency. Adjust the texture as your
baby matures.

4 Serve half immediately. Cover and chill the
remainder and use within 24 hours or freeze
for another meal.

Lentil hotpot

**2 PORTIONS
(9–12 MONTHS)**

Now that your baby is getting older, you can flavour plain lentils by adding onion fried in a little oil or even a small amount of garlic for adventurous tastebuds.

TIP

♦ The addition of a little orange juice provides vitamin C, which aids the absorption of iron from the lentils.

1 teaspoon sunflower oil
2 tablespoons onion, finely chopped
1 carrot, about 125 g (4 oz), rinsed and diced
1 small potato, about 150 g (5 oz), rinsed and diced
½ garlic clove, crushed (optional)
40 g (1½ oz) red lentils, rinsed
200 ml (7 fl oz) homemade vegetable stock or water
2 tablespoons fresh orange juice
1 tablespoon finely chopped fresh chives

1 Heat the oil in a medium saucepan, add the onion and fry for 4–5 minutes until lightly browned. Add the carrot, potato and garlic, if using, then stir in the lentils and stock or water. Bring to the boil, cover and simmer for 25 minutes, topping up with a little extra stock or water if needed.

2 Stir the orange juice and chives into the lentil mixture, then mash or chop to suit your baby.

3 Serve half immediately. Cover and chill the remainder and use within 24 hours or freeze for another meal.

Mediterranean vegetables with quinoa

**2 PORTIONS
(9–12 MONTHS)**

Quinoa is a
South American
alternative to
rice or couscous
and a superior
source of
vegetable
protein. Most
healthfood
shops stock it.

TIPS

♦   Quinoa is the only grain
that provides all the essential
amino acids, making it an
excellent source of protein
for vegetarians. It is also rich
in iron and calcium.

♦   Adding the tomato at the
end of cooking provides
vitamin C and helps to boost
iron and calcium absorption.

1 teaspoon sunflower oil
1 tablespoon finely chopped onion
½ red pepper, cored, deseeded and finely chopped
½ orange pepper, cored, deseeded and finely chopped
½ medium courgette, about 75 g (3 oz), finely chopped
½ garlic clove, finely crushed (optional)
25 g (1 oz) quinoa, rinsed
½ teaspoon tomato purée
300 ml (½ pint) homemade vegetable stock or water
1 tomato, skinned, deseeded and finely chopped
2 teaspoons finely chopped fresh oregano, marjoram
    or basil (optional)

1 Heat the oil in a medium saucepan, add the
onion and fry for 4–5 minutes until lightly browned.
Add the peppers, courgette, and garlic, if using, and fry
for 3 minutes.

2 Stir in the quinoa, tomato purée and stock or water.
Bring to the boil, then lower the heat, cover the pan
and simmer for 20 minutes, or until the quinoa grains
are soft. Add the chopped tomato, and chopped herbs,
if using. Cook, uncovered, for 3 minutes.

3 Mash or chop the mixture to the required texture
for your baby. Serve half immediately. Cover and
chill the remainder and use within 24 hours or freeze
for another meal.

Cheesy polenta with courgettes

1 PORTION (9–12 MONTHS)

As feeding progresses, preparing meals is quicker as you need not purée and seive. Serving soft polenta with a chunkier chopped vegetable sauce is a good halfway meal to encourage your baby towards foods with more texture.

TIPS

◆ Polenta, or coarsely ground cornmeal, provides energy in the form of carbohydrate, protein and minerals, such as iron and potassium. It is a gluten-free grain, suitable for young babies and anyone with gluten intolerance, but check pack labels — some manufacturers coat polenta grains in wheat flour during processing.

◆ Young children need fat as a concentrated form of energy. The best sources are those foods that are rich in other nutrients, such as cheese, which is also rich in protein, calcium and the fat-soluble vitamins A, D, E and K.

1 teaspoon olive oil
50 g (2 oz) courgette, rinsed and finely diced
1 mushroom, rinsed and finely chopped
1 tomato, skinned, deseeded and finely chopped
½ teaspoon tomato purée
150 ml (¼ pint) water
25 g (1 oz) quick-cook polenta
25 g (1 oz) mild Cheddar cheese, grated

1 Heat the oil in a small saucepan, add the courgette and mushroom and fry, stirring, for 2–3 minutes, until very lightly browned. Add the tomato, tomato purée and 3 tablespoons of water. Cover and cook for 5 minutes.

2 Bring the remaining water to the boil in another small saucepan. Sprinkle in the polenta in a steady stream, stirring constantly. Cook over a medium heat, stirring constantly, for 1–2 minutes, until thickened.

3 Stir in the cheese and spoon into a serving bowl. Mash the vegetable sauce, if required. Spoon the sauce on top of the polenta and cool slightly before serving.

Broccoli & fennel risotto

**2 PORTIONS
(9–12 MONTHS)**

This light,
fresh-tasting
one-pot
supper, with
just a hint of
lemon, is quick
and easy to
put together.

TIPS

♦   A risotto base is a good way to introduce your baby to more interesting vegetables and new vegetable combinations.

♦   Broccoli is rich in vitamin C and beta-carotene, and contains some folate, iron and potassium.

♦   Omit the egg if you are following a vegan diet. Boost protein supplies by adding finely chopped tofu, ground toasted hazelnut butter or a sprinkling of ground almonds.

1 teaspoon olive oil
50 g (2 oz) piece of fennel bulb, rinsed and finely
    chopped
50 g (2 oz) risotto rice, rinsed
300–350 ml (10–12 fl oz) hot homemade vegetable
    stock or water
1 egg
75 g (3 oz) broccoli florets, rinsed and cut into tiny
    florets, stems chopped
1 tablespoon lemon juice

1 Heat the oil in a medium saucepan, add the fennel and fry for 2–3 minutes, until softened. Stir in the rice and cook for 1 minute. Add three-quarters of the stock and bring to the boil. Simmer gently, uncovered, for 10 minutes, stirring occasionally.

2 Meanwhile, place the egg in a separate pan of boiling water and cook for 8 minutes to hard-boil. Drain and immerse in cold water, then set aside.

3 Add the broccoli to the rice and moisten with the remaining stock or water, if needed. Cook for 5 minutes, stirring more frequently. Stir in the lemon juice.

4 Spoon half of the risotto into a bowl. Mash or chop if required. Peel the egg and finely chop half of it. Sprinkle it over the risotto in the bowl and serve.

5 Wrap the remaining egg half in cling film and store in the refrigerator. Cover and chill the remaining risotto and use within 24 hours.

Cheat's carrot cassoulet

**2 PORTIONS
(9–12 MONTHS)**

Forget about
long slow
cooking in the
oven, this
speedy
cassoulet
– made with
canned haricot
beans, carrots
and parsnips
– is cooked on
the hob.

TIPS

♦ Pulses are a good source
of protein, minerals, B
vitamins and fibre. This recipe
is an excellent way to
introduce high fibre pulses
into your child's diet in small
amounts so that you don't
overload tiny tummies.

♦ Buy canned beans
without added salt or sugar.
These are usually organic and
sometimes sold in a different
part of the supermarket from
other canned pulses. Home-
cooked dried beans can be
used instead, if preferred.

1 carrot, about 125 g (4 oz), peeled, diced and rinsed
1 small parsnip, about 150 g (5 oz), peeled, diced
    and rinsed
2.5 cm (1 inch) piece green leek, rinsed and thinly sliced
50 g (2 oz) canned haricot beans (without salt or sugar),
    rinsed
few fresh herb sprigs, such as sage, rosemary
    and marjoram
150 ml (¼ pint) homemade vegetable stock or water
1 tomato, skinned, deseeded and finely chopped

1 Put the carrot, parsnip, leek, haricot beans and herb
sprigs into a medium saucepan. Add the stock or
water and bring to the boil, then cover the pan. Lower
the heat and simmer for 15 minutes, until the vegetables
are tender, topping up with extra stock if needed.

2 Add the tomato and cook for a further 2–3
minutes, until softened, then discard the herb sprigs.
Mash or chop the cassoulet for your baby.

3 Serve half immediately. Cover and chill the
remainder and use within 24 hours or freeze for
another meal.

Moroccan lamb

**4 PORTIONS
(9–12 MONTHS)**

Lightly spiced
with just the
tiniest amount
of cinnamon
and garlic, this
slow-cooked
casserole is
the ideal next
step before
joining the rest
of the family
for supper.

TIPS

♦   Even though your baby is
growing up fast, do not use
salty stock cubes for cooking.
If you make your own
homemade stock then you
may prefer to use this
instead, but do not use
homemade stock that has
come from the freezer if you
intend to freeze portions of
this baby dinner.

♦   If you don't have a small
flameproof casserole, prepare
ingredients in a frying pan and
transfer to the smallest
casserole dish that you have,
cover and continue as recipe.

125 g (4 oz) lean lamb steak, trimmed and diced
75 g (3 oz) potato, peeled and diced
75 g (3 oz) carrot, peeled and diced
1 teaspoon olive oil
2 teaspoons finely chopped onion
¼ small garlic clove, crushed (optional)
1 ready-to-eat dried apricot, chopped
1 tablespoon sultanas
pinch of ground cinnamon
½ bay leaf
500 ml (17 fl oz) boiling water
75 g (3 oz) couscous

1 Preheat the oven to 180°C (350°F), Gas Mark 4.
Put the lamb into a sieve, rinse with cold water,
drain well and set aside. Rinse and drain the potato
and carrot. Heat the oil in a small flameproof casserole.
Add the lamb, onion and garlic, if using, and fry, stirring
frequently, for 3 minutes, until browned. Add the potato,
carrot, apricot, sultanas, cinnamon and bay leaf, then
pour in 300 ml (½ pint) of the boiling water. Bring
back to the boil, cover and cook in the preheated
oven for 1 hour.

2 Remove and discard the bay leaf. Reserve a little
stock. Finely chop, mash or process the lamb to the
desired texture, gradually adding the reserved stock,
as needed. Put the couscous into a bowl and pour
over the remaining boiling water. Leave to stand for
5 minutes, then fluff up with a fork and stir into the
lamb. Serve one portion immediately. Cover and chill
the remainder, then pack into 3 small plastic containers,
cover and freeze.

Tuna ragu

4–5 PORTIONS (9–12 MONTHS)

Encourage your baby to try slightly coarser textures by stirring tiny pasta shapes, which are soft and easy to chew, into a smooth, Italian-inspired, mixed vegetable sauce flavoured with a little canned tuna.

TIPS

♦ Use tuna canned in water and not brine, as the latter is far too salty for your baby's digestive system.

♦ For vegetarians, simply omit the tuna and add a little grated cheese.

♦ If you have older children to feed as well, you may prefer to use large pasta shapes and finely chop a portion for the baby.

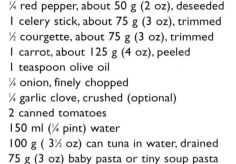

¼ red pepper, about 50 g (2 oz), deseeded
1 celery stick, about 75 g (3 oz), trimmed
½ courgette, about 75 g (3 oz), trimmed
1 carrot, about 125 g (4 oz), peeled
1 teaspoon olive oil
¼ onion, finely chopped
¼ garlic clove, crushed (optional)
2 canned tomatoes
150 ml (¼ pint) water
100 g (3½ oz) can tuna in water, drained
75 g (3 oz) baby pasta or tiny soup pasta

1 Wash the red pepper, celery, courgette and carrot well, drain and finely chop. Heat the oil in a medium saucepan, add the onion and fry, stirring frequently, for 4–5 minutes, until pale golden. Add the garlic, if using, the red pepper, celery, courgette and carrot, cook for 1 minute, then stir in the tomatoes and water. Cover and simmer for 15 minutes, until tender.

2 Pour the mixture into a blender and process until smooth. Finely flake the fish, then stir it into sauce.

3 Half fill a second pan with water and bring to the boil. Add the pasta and cook for 5 minutes, until tender. Drain the pasta, chop if necessary, then stir it into sauce.

4 Reheat one portion and serve immediately. Cover and chill the remainder, then pack into individual plastic containers and freeze.

Eggy bread fingers

**2 PORTIONS
(9–12 MONTHS)**

A great
store-cupboard
standby and
ideal for a
quick late
breakfast, lunch
or tea. It
doesn't matter
if the bread
is slightly
stale, as it will
soon soften
once dipped
in the egg.

TIPS

♦ Keep a watchful eye on young children when they are eating, especially when they begin to feed themselves, as they often forget to swallow and quickly begin to resemble hamsters because of the food stashed in their cheeks.

♦ For a finger food feast, also offer cooked broccoli florets or sticks of cooked carrot.

1 medium egg
2 teaspoons full-fat milk
2 teaspoons sunflower oil
small knob of butter
2 slices bread, crusts removed, halved

1 Beat the egg and milk together in a shallow dish. Heat the oil and butter together in a large frying pan. Quickly dip each piece of bread into the egg mixture and turn to coat. Add to pan and repeat with second slice of bread.

2 Fry for 2–3 minutes, until golden, then turn over and cook the second side for 2–3 minutes. Remove the bread from the pan, cut into finger-size strips. Allow to cool slightly, then serve a few at time.

Tiddler's tortilla

**2–3 PORTIONS
(9–12 MONTHS)**

Another great
store-cupboard
supper and
ideal for babies
of nine months
or over to
share with
older brothers
or sisters. This
simple tortilla
can easily be
adapted to
include a little
diced red
pepper, frozen
sweetcorn,
diced courgette
and a few sliced
mushrooms.

TIPS

♦   Older children may
prefer their omelette with
baked beans or tomato
ketchup, but choose brands
low in, or free from, salt
(sodium) and sugar.

♦   Don't be tempted to add
salt and pepper to foods for
children under one year old.
Add flavour with a little finely
chopped onion, a few chopped
herbs or a little garlic instead.

♦   If you don't have a small
frying pan, use a small,
nonstick saucepan instead,
although it will be a little
more difficult to turn the
tortilla out.

2 teaspoons sunflower oil
125 g (4 oz) cooked potato, diced
2 tablespoons frozen mixed vegetables, large pieces
    chopped
½ spring onion, finely chopped
2 medium eggs
2 tablespoons grated Cheddar cheese

1 Heat the oil in a 15 cm (6 inch) nonstick frying pan.
Add the potato and frozen vegetables and fry over
a gentle heat for 5 minutes, until the potatoes are
browned and the frozen vegetables are hot. Add the
onion and cook for 1 more minute.

2 Preheat the grill. Beat the eggs with the cheese. Pour
the egg mixture into the pan and cook until the
underside is golden. Transfer to the preheated grill,
making sure the pan handle is away from the heat, and
cook until the top of the omelette is golden and the
eggs are thoroughly cooked. Loosen the edge of the
omelette, slide it on to a chopping board and cut into
pieces. Spoon feed your baby or serve as finger food.

Pumpkin & rosemary breadsticks

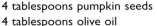

**MAKES 60
(9–12 MONTHS)**

Homemade
breadsticks are
ideal for an
older teething
baby. Freeze,
thawing a few
at a time – they
take about 30
minutes at room
temperature.

TIPS

♦   It is better to encourage
children to snack on savoury
foods rather than sweet ones.
Even babies of nine months
and over will find comfort
chewing on these breadsticks
– especially if they are
troubled with teething.

♦   Pumpkin seeds are a
good source of iron and
phosphorus. They also contain
smaller amounts of potassium,
magnesium and zinc. As the
seeds are finely ground in
these breadsticks, the texture
isn't a problem for babies.

4 tablespoons pumpkin seeds
4 tablespoons olive oil
750 g (1½ lb) strong white bread flour, plus
        extra for dusting
7 g (¼ oz) sachet easy-blend dried yeast
2 tender stems of fresh rosemary, leaves
        very finely chopped
about 500 ml (17 fl oz) lukewarm water

1 Dry-fry the pumpkin seeds in a small heavy-based
frying pan over a medium heat for about 1 minute,
until lightly toasted. Grind the toasted seeds with
2 tablespoons of the oil to a smooth paste in a clean
spice or coffee grinder or with a pestle and mortar.

2 Sift the flour into a bowl, add the pumpkin seed
paste, yeast and rosemary, then mix in enough water
to form a soft, but not sticky dough. Knead vigorously
on a well-floured surface, then cut the dough into 60
pieces. Roll each piece into a 20 cm- (8 inch-) long rope.

3 Preheat the oven to 220°C (425°F), Gas Mark 7.
Lay the dough sticks on 2 large, oiled baking trays,
spacing them slightly apart. Brush lightly with the
remaining olive oil and cover loosely with clingfilm.
Leave in a warm place for about 20 minutes, or until
well risen. Remove the clingfilm.

4 Bake the breadsticks in the preheated oven for
8–10 minutes, transposing the trays after 5 minutes
to ensure even cooking. Transfer to wire racks to cool.

5 Put a few breadsticks in an airtight container and
use within 24 hours. Pack the rest into freezer bags
or one large plastic container, seal and freeze for up to
6 weeks. Take out a few at a time as required.

Cheese straws

These popular snacks are healthier than biscuits or crisps especially if served with raw vegetables.

TIPS

♦ Could use half white and half wholemeal flour, if liked.

♦ Sprinkle straws with sesame seeds if serving to older toddlers.

♦ Try cutting into shapes, letters or animals with biscuit cutters.

125 g (4 oz) plain white flour, plus extra for dusting
50 g (2 oz) butter, diced
75 g (3 oz) mild Cheddar cheese, grated
1 egg yolk
1 egg, beaten

1 Preheat the oven to 200°C (400°F), Gas Mark 6. Put the flour into a bowl, add the butter and rub in with your fingertips or an electric mixer until it resembles fine breadcrumbs. Stir in the cheese. Mix the egg yolk with 1 tablespoon of the beaten egg, stir into the flour and bring together to form a smooth, soft dough.

2 Knead lightly on a floured surface, then roll out to about 3 mm (⅛ inch) thick. Cut into 1 x 5 cm (½ x 2 inch) strips. Brush with the remaining beaten egg, separate the straws and place on a baking sheet, spaced slightly apart.

3 Bake in the preheated oven for 8–10 minutes, until golden. Leave to cool on the baking sheets.

4 Store in a plastic box and use within 2 days or freeze for up to 6 weeks.

Mini apple custard pots

**2 PORTIONS
(9–12 MONTHS)**

Naturally
sweetened
with a little
poached apple,
these small
baked custards
are made
with basic
ingredients
from the larder,
refrigerator
and fruit bowl.

TIPS

♦   Eggs are a good source of
protein and are an important
source of vitamin B12 for
vegetarians. They are also
rich in minerals, including
iron and zinc.

♦ The vitamin C from the
apple aids the absorption of
calcium from the milk.

1 dessert apple, peeled, cored and chopped
1 tablespoon water
pinch of ground cinnamon
butter, for greasing
1 egg
150 ml (¼ pint) full-fat milk

1 Preheat the oven to 180°C (350°F), Gas Mark 4.
Put the apple into a small saucepan with the water
and cinnamon. Cover and cook gently for 5 minutes,
until the apple is soft.

2 Butter 2 ramekins or other small ovenproof dishes
and divide the poached apple between them.

3 Lightly beat the egg in a bowl. Heat the milk in a
pan until just below boiling point, then gradually
beat it into the egg. Strain the custard over the poached
apple in the ramekins.

4 Stand the ramekins in a small roasting tin. Add
boiling water to the tin to come halfway up the
sides of the dishes. Bake in the preheated oven for
20–25 minutes until the custard is set and feels quite
firm to the touch. If it is at all wobbly, return to the
oven for a further 5 minutes.

5 Allow to cool before serving. Use the second
portion within 24 hours. (The custards are not
suitable for freezing.)

Prune & banana sundae

**I SERVING
(9–12 MONTHS)**

If you have a small, hand-held electric baby blender, you can whizz up this delicious, naturally sweet dessert in seconds. It is so quick that you can prepare a single portion as you need it.

TIPS

♦ Bananas are a good source of energy. They are also rich in potassium, which is needed to help regulate the blood.

♦ Prunes are similarly rich in potassium and also contain vitamin B6, iron and fibre. Like bananas, they provide a concentrated form of energy.

♦ Prune juice is low in fibre, but can help to alleviate constipation.

3 ready-to-eat pitted prunes, about 25 g (1 oz)
1 tablespoon fresh orange juice
½ small banana, sliced
2 tablespoons natural bio yogurt

1 Blend the prunes and orange juice together until finely chopped.

2 Add the banana and yogurt and blend briefly, then spoon into a small bowl and serve.

Index

Special Photography
Dave Jordan
Home Economist
Sara Lewis
Executive Editor
Anna Southgate
Editor
Abi Rowsell
Executive Art Editor
Leigh Jones
Designer
Mike Leaman
Copy Editor
Linda Doeser
Proof reader
Lesley Malkin
Picture Researcher
Jennifer Veall
Production Controller
Jo Sim